"Jason Baldinger's *American Aorta* pulses like a midwestern road trip to the dustbowl, the soundtrack a steady thump of pavement and beating sun. You can smell the diesel and fast food on your fingers and in your clothes. "In a roadhouse/I order a gallon of sweet tea/a platter of catfish/let the air conditioner be my spine." Baldinger brings us to each new scene with largehearted compassion and tender observation. From "painkillers and double shift towns" and "for miss woodchopper" to "emphysema highways" and "bonnie parker heart", characters are sketched here from dust and rust, their souls on subtle display. This collection is a lifetime of travel and connection through the American rustbelt with gracious tribute at each stop, asking its readers to return, to savor the words like a slow sun laying itself wide at the edge of the sky. "After the speakeasy/stars pour molten metal/sparks of rustbelt towns/fade in a kansas city skyline… as the hours flash on/age plays tag with us."

-Jonie McIntire, Poet Laureate of Lucas County, Ohio (2022-2024), author *Semidomesticated* (1st edition, Red Flag Poetry 2020 chapbook contest winner; second edition Sheila-Na-Gig Editions, 2022)

Also by Jason Baldinger:

The Whiskey Rebellion w/ Jerome Crooks (Six Gallery Press)
The Lady Pittsburgh (Speed and Briscoe Press)
The Lower Forty-Eight (Six Gallery Press)
The Studs Terkel Blues (Nightballet Press)
Fumbles Revelations (Grackle and Crow)
This Useless Beauty (Alien Buddha Press)
The Ugly Side of the Lake w/ John Dorsey (Nightballet Press)
The Better Angels of our Nature (Kung Fu Treachery Press)
Blind into Leaving (Analog Submission Press)
A Threadbare Universe (Kung Fu Treachery Press)
The Afterlife is a Hangover (Stubborn Mule Press)
The Nu Profit$ of P/O/E/T/I/C Di$chord: *And Even if we
Did, So What!?* (OAC Book w/ Damian Rucci,
Shawn Pavey, Nathaniel Stolte
A History of Backroads Misplaced: Selected Poems 2010-2020
(Kung Fu Treachery)
Little Fires Hiding w/ James Benger (Kung Fu Treachery Press)
Everyone's Alone Tonight w/ James Benger (Kung Fu Treachery Press)
This Still Life w/ James Benger (Kung Fu Treachery Press)
Topography of Disappearing (Between Shadows Press)
Don't Spook the Armadillo (La Belle Riviere Press)
Lazarus (Photographs) (OAC Press)

american aorta

Poems by Jason Baldinger

OAC Press
Belle, MO

Copyright © Jason Baldinger 2023

First Edition: 1 3 5 7 9 10 8 6 4 2

ISBN: 978-1-958182-43-7

LCCN: 202339120

Cover image: Jon Dowling

Interior image: Jason Baldinger

Author photo: Alanna Teach Crow

Acknowledgments:

some of these poems have appeared in *lunch bucket brigade,
red fez, trailer park quarterly, as it ought to be, poetrybay, the rye
whiskey review, winedrunk sidewalk, vox populi, gasconade review,
fearless, sledgehammer, riverdog, rustbelt review, anti-heroin chic, alien
buddha zine, seppuku, mad swirl, live nude poems*, as well as the
anthologies: *back of the class presents: not ready for the river styx
& nu prophets of poetic dischord: and even if we did, so what*

portions of this book come from the chapbooks *the
topography of disappearing* (between shadows press) and *don't
spook the armadillo* (la belle riviere press)

Table of Contents

away you rolling river

shenandoah
traditional

american aorta

temporal, temporary and gone

it's black out in bar harbor
days after a thanksgiving prayer
was spoken with no meaning

it's offseason and sunday
few residents creak
through a vacant glaze
the early arrival of pitch black
stars not shielded by light

I follow a fiddlehead fern
south to a trout hatchery
where generations of tourists feasted
fifty cents for each wild caught dream
perfectly broiled over an open fire
picnic benches for the family while you wait

next month, i'll be miles down coast
walking rehoboth beach with wine stains
fireworks explode dolle's taffy orange
I turn my back on the breakers
footprints already washed away

this infinite space
stoned and stealing time again
the new year a dragon slayed at my feet

these places, theses years whisk by
sand in my beard
atoms dispersed in air
no meaning in moments anymore
it all builds to a crescendo
I'll never hear

tonight, memories flood
a mad swirl of stations
some past, some present, some future
temporal, temporary and gone

I, psychedelic voyager

the mountain valley diner
van morrison is *blowing your mind*
but this reality is more *t.b. sheets*

virgil, wayne royo
nested in fifties decor
amazed as I map
the roots, the nerves
under my teeth
on a napkin

amazed as I stop time
while the waitress waits
to trade an acapella *thunder road*
for a chocolate shake

I've spent too much time
in battle or bar crawl
brain full of brewer's yeast
while body suited regulars
shake booties hypnotic

it's hot in this tent
the next wounded soldier
gets whiskey and a bit for their teeth
then one breath before the saw
a slow symphony of screams

trail riders mount fresh horses
they remember the day
john brown took on harper's ferry
somehow one-hundred and fifty years on
I still see dangerfield newby die
everyday on the internet

by the time I get to gettysburg
virgil will need to drive
those big rig lights and solar flares
damn my eyes

I see the way you jumped at me
lord from behind the door

it takes lifetimes
to disavow the existence of god
unless you live a war
or a season at the edge of america

I know a bar outside the new year
where armies of tvs are dark
let's slip into our dotage
give in to the interstate
let's disappear

american aorta

we meditate on a dead fish
carcass clean to bone
still as the mississippi flows
american aorta

my trucker tan, lobster red
arm wrapped in black t-shirt
highway 61 through this native land
of bobby zimmerman
and the sioux
spirits rise from asphalt heavy as july
there is no air conditioning the midwest

my co-pilot has had enough
ping pong of cities
languid humidity
she lets me handle haze
all the way to a cinder block
motel outside the quad cities

I slid in a disc
bought in minneapolis
out of print gem unearthed
michael hurley
the unholy modal rounders
have moicy!
inch volume

robbin' banks
motor at top speed
as years inherited
in the sway of this river
dissipate

perfect soundtrack forever
the broken pottery and depression glass
in the heart of the heartland

I chance waking her
nicotine fingers tap the wheel
replay, I sing along under my breath
fancy that outlaw life
so intertwined with this rugged mythology
thresher wind pushes us down the highway
I love being illegal

these blue veins

(for lilly portage)

there's a copy of *leaves of grass*
aging in the back window of my saturn
cover sun bleached
dog-eared torn, toned
with car windows open
pages wriggle free to blow
in the wind of these blue veins

I brought walt along for ceremony
2012, day two of seventy-five
cross country get downs
as dennis hopper asked
what is america?

in that green corner of harleigh cemetery
we read whitman at whitman
as he brushed whisps of the civil war's hair

I tramp a perpetual journey
look for the soul in this lost nation
look for myself in mirrors of maps
strewn across the front seat

walt has traveled with me since
a talisman over these endless miles
where everything is lost

in the weight of the moment
where every city fades
in the full throat of the rear view

I can't count all the small town stars
the fireworks and sunsets
all the loneliness found
across these blue veins

like that years pass
I'm standing in a car wash
vacuuming a saturn for one last ride
holding this abused talisman

I can't throw it out
it carries weight
how sweet the silent backward tracings

the next longest train

you may say it was laudanum
that led alexander creel to believe
the virgin mary was standing
on the banks of the ohio
past a river island
in a land then called virginia
even though it was probably
a mothman
a thunderbird
or a blur in the bright of steam

I mean laudanum was all the rage
ask merriwether lewis
who was shooting bears in his night shirt
before he internalized that muzzle loader
making a mess of the walls of an inn
in grinders switch
which is still in tennessee

coal dust chokes summer sun
the next longest train
I ever saw rattles down main
it's 245 in the afternoon
heaped cars stretch long past
the food giant sign
that adorns the hardware store

I sip sweet tea on a bench
engine disappears
into wetlands at the edge of town

this is where I live now
in the shadow of history
in the shadow of a coal train
somewhere in a portal
between past and present
the future lost or locked away
wish I could say the view
was anything but bleak

george washington slept here

sink in mud to the ankle
the moment you wash
off the tailgate

across empty campground
otter creek swollen
brown rising bed

mountains dressed in rain
maybe a town will change this luck

chrome fixtures warm coffee
waitress with a sly smile
then back to rain
in narrow alleys
the old city market

we flipped quarters
for a next destination
while waiting for our bacon

heads
we keep it south another hour
if we can't find clear skies we'll try west

washington comes up
three outta three

and not in drag like cincinnati

weather rights itself

south of danville

washington never slept

west of johnson city anyway

this poem was written for john dorsey
in the el bronco bar,
richmond indiana

chill as fuck
across gossamer ohio
through endless western sunset

babe, I'm sorry it was you
cancer took to the prom
when friends hear you're together
they freeze in existential headlights

brother, I'm sorry that grief
doles out shitty drunk lap dances
no care if those duckets
ever roost in a g string

john, I promise fried chicken
and all world shaking doom allows
in less time than a waffle house day

I'll be on the horn to gus's
soon as I kill the engine
in the sky high pie parking lot
maplewood is an armadillo away

over dinner the other night
I said magic and loss

I say it often, in and out of context
a friend replied, with enough time served
magic doesn't hold sway over
the ocean of loss we worship at now

I can't say I disagree
except the waitress who calls
me amigo like I've never left
just delivered a grande margarita

in the hum of three hundred easy miles
and the shine of tequila
I won't want to buy a camper

but I have the receipt for short walk
in lights between speedway and meijer
lights that stretch from here
as far as midwest wherever
you know I'll be there soon

let go of atlantis

jerry believes in ivory soap
he believes in starched collars
his spine is straight, he says
all the flying plagues
of florida are near sited
don't give them room to smell

I missed the manatees
out in some cove near
the launch pad that's etched
in our consciousness
I see rockets in the rearview
and I want to write about
shoveling snow as a boy
about dreams exploding
about hot cocoa
and christa mcauliffe

jerry says for fifteen bones
they'll give me a sea kayak
I can paddle over surf
to a barrier island all my own

out there cooking hamburger
helper over a pocket rocket
Ill turn back/ahead time
ill forget my couth and go native

going native is a racist term
meant to minimize
the people who were killed
so this land could be our land
a universe of violence

it seems that every inch
of this land is steeped in blood
I wonder if a barrier island
off the coast of the atlantic
may be one of the few places
I can step where that blood
doesn't well up, a hot spring
of unacknowledged history

I'm gonna stay out here
an island a mile away from civilization
the sun paints the sky every twelve hours
every day the ocean steps a little higher
when it reaches my neck
I'll know its time
to let go of atlantis

last stand with a vagrancy charge

(for damian rucci)

what would ray carver say about us
rowdier than blue springs can muzzle
the main street dust
malt in the milkshake
kansas city close enough
you hear parker
blare *ornithology* down 18th

you hear diz shouting
salt peanuts salt peanuts
in the stockyards, this ain't no
kerouac trip, but he knew
bop was the only true
american revolution

I want to vote gillespie in 64
I want to still be sitting here come spring
watch the monarchs rise
boys of summer stare down october

what would ray carver say
through his hangover
we're sitting on a park bench
staring down shift change
the last stand with a vagrancy charge
that's the highest honor
street poets can be afforded

time went the way of the buffalo

(for diane wahto)

I know wichita
from a gas station
overlooking the interstate

a jaw dropping sunrise over flint hills
I pulled my hoodie against october

with eight hundred miles ahead
one last gasp of wichita
before wagons west

it's sad we never met
we should have had breakfast
but time went the way of the buffalo

I would have loved to hear in person
your story of marching
five miles in kalamazoo

you and your friend
against the vietnam war
you and your friend
all dressed up in high heels

painkillers and double shift towns

she works mornings at kroger
cashier ringing orders
everyone she went to high school with
everyone else that got stuck

she leaves her daughter at daycare
later grandmother picks up granddaughter
afternoons after her job
takes her home plants her in front of the tv

she leaves kroger for evening shifts
waiting at the bbq pit downtown

her grandmother falls asleep
while grandaughter plays in front of the tv
morgan's raid like the civil war came to nothing

the men in this town are trash
they stink of the failure found
under the thumb of an american dream

we know it's bullshit
but have you ever tried
to convince yourself out of
some kind of propaganda

she's all eyes as I finish my second beer
I've been sleeping on the ground all week
I like the attention

she rests her hip on my shoulder
pronounces my name off card flirting
she has the giggles

I'll debate a minute waking up
in a room disheveled
in that two jobs and single mom way
in that she'll never catch-up way

I think about her pouring cereal and milk
trying to get her daughter to eat
before rushes for drop off
another day of a pair of shifts
another day too tired
work and TV and sleep
automation

I'll tuck my wallet
shuffle out the front door
she's crying on the steps
next to the cook
overwhelmed

I'll spend the night
counting spiders
in o'bannon's woods

in the morning

I'll follow this river west

through painkillers and double shift towns

the ohio is only water

it can't save anyone

for souls in need of relief

chase a season dying
over myriad stretches
of backroad no place

fifteen years ago
nothing was solid
I was two jobs clinging
to the edge of forgotten

trying like hell to find myself
in a pack a day
a six pack a night
and sixty hours a week
if your lucky you find bottom

I scrapped enough for a road trip
three days across
the grand army of the republic highway
but who thinks of the grand army anymore
with its glory glory hallelujah

the pennsylvania wilds
in a car with a broken tape deck
two stations fuzz locations
modern country or christian radio
neither provide comfort
for souls in need of relief

muffler men grim reapers
the worst college bars
smoking cigarettes in bungalows
while streams wash by
this is not escaping

the years leave memories
raw as place
here they claim freedom
shout *the sky is falling*
hell, maybe it is

at the gas station
a man with sunken eyes
skin pallid enough
to suggest a final destination
says the jake brake is locked
all night coffee and grease
he still won't make delivery on time
he'll still be pulling chain
when harrisburg comes due at nine

copperheads

eating fried plantains cold
in a morning motel
in a town burned by the confederacy

if I drive east
fifty-one thousand skeletons
rest in pieces underground

if I follow antietam creek south
I'll find twenty thousand more

still, as I follow these roads
I find symbols of a fallen
illegitimate government
hanging everywhere

sometimes next to the flag
of the country it tried to secede from
as if it's possible to carry two
divergent systems to the well of democracy

sometimes it flies alone
or with colonial flag pairing
don't tread on me
as if two widely different
revolutions meant the same thing

in one case it was inside an american flag
like a superman s
like a hidden heartbeat
that's maybe the most accurate

this is pennsylvania
there were no copperheads here
until now

america, your wars are endless
but none is longer than the one
you've had with yourself
still there is no shining city
your ideals are empty
all epaulets and piping

these future sons and daughters
of the confederacy they play victim
in a system failed

they side with those that exploit
in a system built to exploit

although I'm a student of history
I've lost my taste for war
civil or otherwise

there is no glory in dying
there is less in exploitation
I don't know how to tell that

to the ghosts that wade in the blood
rivulets that once rushed to creeks

johnny reb
the cause is lost
my eyes are tired
tired of seeing the glory
of the coming of the lord

there is still no vintage
in grapes, in wrath
just a terrible swift sword
this truth is stumbling
there is no marching on

when pigs fly

maybe pigs will fly
take a running start down st nicolas
into the wind like early sons of aviation
before crashing into the monongahela

maybe they'll launch from wadell avenue
a doppler squeal lost in a mothball sky
in this valley of work anything is possible
even the great american dream

stan musial could flat out hit
from the back of the batters box
bat sweeping across the plate
ball bouncing off left field wall
he hustles into second

he worked off seasons
a freight checker at u.s. steel
his wife set up housekeeping
a few blocks from where he was born
maybe the world was smaller then

they were off to st louis
when the inversion started
smog veils, this valley nightmare
gossamer sunsets
halloween gas masks
a weight that sits
suffocating on your chest

it was no surprise
people started to die

it was no surprise doom
settled this city in smog
musial collected his parents
sent them to enjoy their dotage
somewhere in suburban missouri

he didn't come back
not to sit on a jeep on thanksgiving
as parades death marched
from the sons of italy
past the rooming houses
as hills knife down river

to forbes field
cardinals in traveling grays
musial sends bob friend's fastball
on a right field richochet
clemente fields it cleanly
fires it home
musial at second
tips his hat as pigs fly by

the valley of work gasps for breath
the rich will always get richer
the air may recover
really, it's more lottery than dream

that night in buffalo

that night in buffalo
his last poem, his last lines
he tore his book in half
walked into the mouth
of a summer night
lighter sparks pages

the audience still
on their hands
stunned silence
the malaise
of middle age boredom

dude on the radio
sings some sad dog
white boy boogie
the end of the world
live streamed
from topanga canyon
in the seventies
he sounds all teeth chatter
and crispy cocaine daze

last sip of daydream
high life is warm
there is no lighter fluid
left to burn this afternoon down
everything comes to ashes eventually

that night in buffalo
we were in the pool
except him in a deck chair
rattling through his schemes
                        his interrogations
as if one more story
could keep him just ahead of his past

damn the whirlwind came alive
in my living room
her threats to tear his throat out
probably with her teeth
as he cowered behind a door

he disappeared the next day
bank statements drained in boxed wine
debt collectors sent howler monkeys
he tried to leave no trace

that winter smelled like a campfire
his trail swept off in central pennsylvania snow
a new enemies list to burn
at the finale of that next never show

this time sparrows fly out

it's been a year since
I woke up in nashville
on the floor of a revolution
that couldn't be seen
on the floor with chipmunks
sparrows, the smell of fall
in the dead leaves of an old hickory tree

here we are with all this loss
her hands no longer turn to crows at dawn
her old lover dead
she has guilt, she has resentment
you can build a life there
but goddamn it isn't a place
any of us could, or should, stay

watch the conversation turn to anxiety
this is what we talk about when we talk about now
so adieu false heart

now let me open my hands
this time sparrows fly out
will overwhelm a world of beech trees

our illnesses are myriad in this light
goddamn, are as tired as I am
do you find the word *tomorrow*

heavy as damp stars
does it seem strange to you
when you say tomorrow
it's like it's already here, like it'll never arrive
say it with me now, it might be alright

we pray angels met you on the shore

don't know about your apocalypse
but I'm running out end times
shuddering down a dirt mountain road
in a new used car I paid cash
on the barrelhead for
dust cloud in the rear view
rises with morning mist

keep alternating whiplash
juice gas then brake
that drop off
into the creek
gives me the side eye

I'm sniffing out a trail head
trying to find a mountain
to dose space dust with

I hear it before I smell it
goddamn those old mother mountains
are whistling *o danny boy*
evidently every damn word
etched in my dna
sing along, try not to get myself
weepy eyed melancholy
then it dawns on me
that ain't the fucking mountains

it's an *actual* set of bagpipes
sweet and sour tone all over
this rushing morning stream

sun clears that side of the mountain
blind a moment
slow to realize
I am locking eyes
with a goddamn bagpipe playing bigfoot

I've watched the patterson-gimlin film
I'm in no way starstruck
this is another awkward moment
in a lifetime of them
there's nothing more to see
than notes floating in dust
we pray that angels met you on the shore

a carrollton prayer

(for victor clevenger)

parked in a convertible
cadillac on a side street
under a cottonwood
to shade the missouri sun
sprawled across the seat
raconteur in aviators
looking john prine
and sweet revenge
but prine like so many things
these past years is gone

I was tired of watching beehives
shop in the shadow of james shields
I stopped in the five and ten
they didn't need a stranger
and I didn't need a job

when we stumbled into each other confused
how exactly I did I get to the where of here
all these small towns look the same

we should head for the homestead
a field of clevengers growing on the plains
des moines, kansas city
just far enough away

we could drop in some
cinder block lounge
where they boil hotdogs all day
catch the high life
as cigarette smoke
resembles eisenhower's profile

we could head southwest
through the wizard of oz panhandles
where stockyards reek of death
even with the semi's rocketing past
that smell sticks well past dalhart

we could talk lester madden
how it's all come to sharks

instead it's health insurance
the mundane features
that staple into a life
how this could be ohio
or georgia or 1983
it's all the same moment
no matter which america you see

peter laughner's ghost

(for john burroughs)

it begins with chicken paprikash
touching elbows with strangers
sharing tables in this tiny diner

the woman is waiting
for her friend after church
before going to care for her mother
like pittsburgh the women of cleveland
are tough gnarl blizzards howling
across this post-industrial landscape

they still cough mill smoke
carry traditions, novenas
I have my traditions too
we're all just getting by

i'll be here again
waiting to get snowed in
on van gogh's birthday
from white out to motel
I float like peter laughner's ghost

george avenue will always be sacred
john, shelley and the dogs
up into magic hours
with an internet jukebox

and stories of our appalachian lives
the marks it's left on our souls

we practice moderation as we get older
still, as americans we feel
we are imbued with some strange light

this morning, light sits in smoke
the vapor of exhaust
we are hungry for stories

it ends with chicken paprikash
our memories fading

for rivers that have heard it all before

to wake on a wrap around mirror
this third floor walk up closet
a stone's throw from the ancient dead

it's all gray ghosts
as morning breathes storm clouds
I'm still looking for the right words
for rivers that have heard it all before

now it's ohio again
after bourbeuse and wabash
after missouri's north fork utopia
after the gasconade's grieving
after st genevieve's cloak
stretched from paris on the seine
to this mississippi, mother of waters
only a river can make things right

a pocket of quarters to tip a taqueria
while oldham county puts
on its new courthouse face

train smoke billows
muddies curved glass main streets
as if americana was still a thing

I guess it's the snakes that got me
slithering wind, eating highways
the accelerator a struggle
miles adding up to time
the little deaths
the neon rest stops
the process of gaining
just to lose again

it's like I'm stuck
in the lunch rush of vandalia
wearing lincoln's stove pipe
listening to a disc jockey
read the weekend's funerary announcements again

deep elem blues

(for paul koniecki)

I've never seen dallas
from a DC-10 at night
but the saw that floats
through that flatlanders song
is every phantom embodied
across the miles
lubbock to wichita falls

I've never taken the 287 ramp
followed highways into the zapruder film
now history is a butthole surfers video

alan dulles was wholly responsible
for kennedy's assassination
for america's second bloody coup

he was killed because the cuban missile crisis
had turned him from hawk to chicken hawk
it tore his spine out
left him with a world
longing for peace

revenge and capitalism
can't survive peace
hence lee harvey oswald
hence jack ruby

hence what really happened
on the grassy knoll
can carry its weight in mystery

paul, I headed for texarkana
because sometimes the road
offers no salvation
sometimes the wheels
are another form of madness

we should be smoking joints
in the back yard of oswald's rooming house
you'd look at me as larry levis and say
so death blows his little
fucking trumpet big deal

I'd answer as phil levine
I can hear the even breathing
of all that is wordless and final

the butthole surfers play
the shah sleeps in lee harvey's grave
maybe our preachin' days are through
cause when the night dusts off those tejas stars
fuck if I don't fall hard into the deep elem blues

blue ridge crashes

a wave of blue ridge crashes
palmetto bugs scatter in ornamental beds
gunpowder lightning sky
pop pop and thunder ricochets
across apple orchards
I'm not sure which of battles
for winchester I've stumbled in

let me break away
those mother mountains call
I've got a mockingbird on either shoulder
a mimosa branch in either hand
I'm flailing
trying to reach the sky
above a scorched green sea

I want nothing more
than patsy cline
singing shenandoah
her voice louder
than imagination
or cannonade

along the ridge
above the rock farms
I stretch beyond lightning
catch a breeze

maybe not soaring

something like gliding

something like a turkey vulture dying

mr clarinet
(for ben shahn)

here's to anxiety mr clarinet

I never thought this would be

the first or the last day in the garden

eden is mid-winter detroit

we're playing shuffleboard

cold pint glasses

grains of sand

adam and eve

at it on the couch

eve straddling adam

the dry hump olympics

lasts more than one beer

mr clarinet maybe you could draw

down your knotted hands

bring up your horn

its reed on fire

blow something

to make us think

about how we'll feel

when times dies

remind us that with all

the careful construction of mythology

that god has failed

mr clarinet, bring up the horn
with the scary clowns
play an elegy
that sounds like jimmy giuffre
chasing raymond scott
while adam and eve
swallow static sparks
penance is always eviction

mr clarinet the anxiety is real every day
in or out of the garden

eve has dismounted
she is smoothing fabric
adam is bowlegged
you're right to keep your hands
covering up this horror

adam and eve
walk into an exiled night
when we finish our beers, we'll do the same
not one fucking snake in sight

the high and hundred proof choir

legs hang from a sky
choked out in deep black
it's threatened since dayton
hang on hydroplane
the torrents come
other side of the state line

this bar is overrun with roughnecks
road crew yellow shirts stained
evening happy hour spirals into night

slurs, bravado
exchange punches across the bar
these working man's things

blonde secretary runs the jukebox
senior prom hits from a decade ago
back when day jobs were nightmares
only parents talked about

outside it's howling
a road crew knows
each drink that takes today's pain
starts tomorrow's deficit

they fall off stools
into autopilot drunk drives

into bed, as they muster
they whisper a prayer to weather

I'll pray tonight
with the high and hundred proof choir
let the rain come
let the jobs and roads wash away
let us all sleep deep into the infinity
of an unexpected three-day weekend
these savored gifts braced against a hangover's pain

the only other thing is nothing

(for will hackney)

got your postcard from the edge of civilization
in a resort town where water
stopped like time in the shimmer of 118 degrees
out where the sea level can't find the sea

california has eluded me
I haven't seen the salton sea
but I miss zabriske point
I miss armed attendants
pumping priceless gas
under blazing mojave sun
desert rats aware apocalypse already flashed

the last time we shared a desert
you were celebrating life beginning
as speeches and dances rolled
I was in the parking lot
cold moon rises full over the sierra blanca

attempts to be a dutiful
if long distanced partner
lonely in the clash
between living with abandon
and living abandoned

I am yucca, sun bleached
blossoms mummified
while she's hostile
brandishing the shovel
that would bury us

come morning
I start east
eyes on lubbock

beyond roswell
I spy a pecan grove
symmetrical oasis stretches forever
park between rows
stand outside myself
the only other thing is nothing

I remember the royal river

I remember the royal river
a bleached skeleton
bones calloused and raw
these forever miles
the only skin left attached
vermont rain soaked halos
glow dry in cold july sun

I remember the royal river
mile long rutted driveways
a peninsula breaks into islands
black flies, tall grass
backgammon days pass
picking ticks off golden retrievers

I remember the royal river
the maine granite coast
lone trees claw to hold rocks
the ice cold atlantic
this gaunt face in tide pool

I remember the royal river
tequila on the docks
fortification for a last days boogie
gather these atoms south
with notions of sacco and vanzetti

I remember the royal river

as a skeleton

with a compass

left in place

of memory

mile high sasquatch

my uncle drove trucks all his life
assuming his life started
after he left vietnam

we haven't talked in years
but he and his truck driver son
tell stories riddled with routes
read between the lines
even numbers and north
it all went to shit
odd numbers and south
there's no permanence to anything
if you wanna wrestle east or west
you better have a full beer
and something hard for chaser

I wonder if like me
he fell in love one night
in a morehead kentucky motel
only to be estranged by chillicothe
maybe for him it was
hue to da nang

I never asked
as he only speaks about
the war in racism and bravado
the way he was trained

I wonder if like me
he sat on a mountain
above a ghost town
alternating tired feet
in an ice cold steam
laughing madman
or mile high sasquatch
breathing in every cloud
in a chilled spring sky

maybe it's as ho chi mihn said
men and animals rise up reborn
what could be more natural

robert mitchum said
the snakes are my friends
he said it with weariness
the weariness of a person who carries
more than their weight in miles

a wishbone of cottonwood

all hang dog hungover
after party roared thru magic hours
crash on parlor floor
peck at sleep

awake 8am silence
a wishbone of cottonwood
drags iron avenue remains
looking for whatever truth
can be scratched with a nail
              harbored on a lens

heaven is a donut shop
as billboards crow
hysterectomies your way

next time you see me
I'll be wrapped in pool table felt
all night grazing at ihop

skyscraper waitress leaves
a joke on the check
in slippery careful pink
something about cinnamon buns

maddie
desperados are waiting with airline tickets

take your tips
clean out the register
run till past where the prairie meets eternity
you know this place is dyin'
there is no shame now in gettin' gone

ageless broken hearts

I write too many poems
about the rustbelt
too many words
for my ex-patriot friends
shunned in the diaspora of closed
now torn down steel mills
about the nihilism this version
of america has always been

I'm reminded of another apocalypse
teddy roosevelt rifle in hand
a week unknown and off the reservation
stalking buffalo that once ruled these plains
it took a week to get one in the sights
he admired it momentarily
shot it promptly
put down his rifle and cried

that story is probably bullshit
like wading through a seven am sunrise
in a diner window overlooking
the carbon snow of another nameless town
in another winter of death and discontent
with another waitress pouring coffee
too weak to defend itself

if this place were real we'd expect

florence martus to start

waving ships back into port

the prettiest girl in savannah dies everyday

another victim in a long line of ageless broken hearts

we settled for ann arbor

it was easy to think you had it all
on a rock, in a creek
her soprano draped around arias
maria callas mingles in oak leaves
sun blind bright across water
every second a lightning flash

but she was wobbly
not that I wasn't too
always on a precipice
over the entirety of our weeks

I wanted to chase fall somewhere
another stab, keep this kinetic
thing from prying apart
we settled for ann arbor

her saturday dj shift wrapped at 6 am
I follow radio waves until we hit light speed
four hours and michigan

trust jesus, trust jesus, trust jesus
bridge footers repeat this kingdom's command

touchdown rain dance as wolverines leave the field

traffic bleeds from a wound named november

we wade deep in record store afternoons

how many trout were lost on huron avenue?

she said something about aurora borealis

as we cross the dark endless ohio

the prosperity social club

state college
last motel to swallow
after seventy days or forty-five thousand miles
this warranty polished in blue highway lexicon

near enough pittsburgh
stations static homesick
who needs one last reading
let's gun it for the homestead

the reverend is on a greyhound though
i'll find him in a basement
sharing a jim beam neat
with a mural of chief wahoo

tremont is hidden magic
I can't find the golden spell though
guided by semaphore it's no surprise we're late

this audience is first appearances of rustbelt poets
welcome to the topography of disappearing

after our words fade
after all conversations extinguish
we leave prosperity social club
dressed for the high life

the last hundred drenched in biblical rain
race the hydroplane as lightning strobes along
flaming lips stereo
will I see the lady pittsburgh again?

tunnel opens to electric heaven
now enter the bardo
as friends cheer my arrival
wet and dusty and ecclesiastical
in a pink death oubliette
where cigarette smoke gained sentience

it's past midnight
grant has taken vicksburg
I'm thirty-six now
no understanding of who I've become

alcohol cleaves this addled brain
the leaving rains hard as before
shirt off into the wee hours
a madman, a shell, a demon
all free and unhinged madness

the blood of a highway song

sky fills with light
even as days lungs
fumble for breath

a symphony of robins
of pee wees, of titmice and jays
act as tourniquet
slow the blood of a highway song

nested in an unripe blueberry patch
fruit late season green
humidity and dew for a blanket

I appear as newborn faun
I appear as satyr
then shift to crow
before regaining shape as a man

this happens when roads
in the blood finally win
when the delaware water gap
is another broken heart
when one too many sunsets
throw poems into a man-made lake

mosquitoes swarm in vengeance
sharks in the estuary

fins above the surface
trumpet the dark nostalgia of 1916
nightmares under glass waves glimmer
a traffic jam across mini-mall tundra

to kiss the ocean in a moment
in the mirror of motion
then dissipate as vapor
another city, another town
the summer sun a demon

an effingham prayer

interstate pinned to motel door
full moon tap dances
my lover a burial mound of pillows
sleeps through this sea of noise

it's that night in effingham again
after hangover readings in st louis
poets forever from home

shania, blonde angel receptionist
suggests coupons
we camped on mcgowin's dime

dorsey set to work
on chainsaw sculptures
the semi's, the travelers
the all night interstate ballet
I give into earplugs
drift to restless

we are constant motion
hummingbirds, poets, lost souls
left miles from anything
left to catch voices
floating in this kinetic space

all of this is magic
like finding a case
of redbreast on the balcony
bow on top
the note shouts
drink up pittsburgh!

among the rustbelt undead

the memory of your passing
wafts across social media this morning
I play one of your songs
eleven distorted roaring minutes
everyday is another stupid miracle

the silent shouts of my phone
in the fog of that january night
sleeplessness led to weariness
disconsolate drives along thick grey pastures
before the coming of mountains
cold blast of open windows kept me steady

behind the wheel this morn
I trace these river roads
tarry among the rustbelt undead
under a sky martyred between
cooling towers, methane crackers
those sharp plumes toxic white
the orange runoffs into ohio

desolate arteries of forgotten frozen towns
a man stops me on the street
in a high ohio valley nasal whine
t'is tahns ded, inn't

I look around a second
clouds reflected in windows
this has to be a simulation
I nod, mumble, sure is
the truth is far more grim
rust flecks animated
blood in a snow globe
the endlessness of neglect

pretty boy floyd is stuck
a fly with wings coated in newsprint
I turn inland, follow headlines
to the tune of october 22, 1934

your wife texts
with offers of beer and burgers
company to salve this loneliness
I'm hours away from anywhere
still at a strip mall red light
a sign stares back with little grace
you can't break a city forged in steel

the oxbow on the sheepscot

ocean point sunset
then the christmas lights of booth bay
and shrines for the dead
lost in the empty expanse of a pizza shop

he sports a fu manchu
through thirty years of photos
the wall remembers
his daughters work the counter
a greek sisterhood blessed
heredity offers the same nose

I've got a cold bottle of coke
watching the down jackets
and duck boots grab
an easy pre-holiday meal
ice down the stress until tomorrow

the last table reserved
for the virgin mary and the dead
photos with prayer candles
I match the photos
then watch them disappear
slowly fading in the current of time

I'm waiting to hear my name
so I can shuffle into the night

white box on the front seat
through glowing lichen dark
find the oxbow on the sheepscot
that lies beyond the last dream
blue sand still on my boots

metaphysics of a skeleton

there is nothing to do in great falls
on a sunday before the season
except listen to water roar

six weeks on the road
I am the metaphysics of a skeleton
the road picked me clean

in an antiseptic motel
I, taco connoisseur
deal in the worst
del, john and sol
99 cent dyspepsia

this is the place we lose track of narrative
as if all those dinosaurs buried under
the surface have influence as they fade to fossil

here on blacktop disappearing
with endless open miles
I am already gone
these mountains they continue to wither
the sky still looks for its reflection
trying to focus through the wind, the grass and the dust

that ben hur life

the interstate chariot race
an empty competition
there is no salvation in beating a gps
no horse shit just roadkill
if your lucky you may find
white jesus waving an american flag
calling racers to pit
o that ben hur life

me, I prefer green corn
acres eye high deep in july
red winged blackbirds
watch over two lanes
watch waves across the sea

12:15, I didn't follow orange detours
I made my own inventory
of one stop sign towns
odell, linden, romney

god bless america amplifies
across crawfordsville haze

o kate smith
let's get earnest
across those fruited plains
until gray asphalt gives out
in an ocean white with foam

I have hours to go
to drift under the current
of a future harvest
there's a thunderstorm
in my pocket for safe keeping
maybe I'll dust it off come the next state line

for patrick beard and the rusty razors

this poem is for patrick beard and the rusty razors
who played barefoot on one leg
to an empty bar on a red river tuesday

my last name got recognized
it had nothing to do with a candy store
as I walk down 6th
sunday afternoon cheers echo
my cousin centers the line
while danny white gets ghosted by history

irma thomas covers
rattle the windows
duck in for a beer
the next venue
the next beer
repeat til neon swims
repeat til patrick beard the rusty razors
finish their first set to an empty bar

I've played to empty rooms
read to scatters of tumbleweeds
in more places I can count
it's a sobering experience

I can't leave empty bars while a band plays
if there is no one to witness did these moments exist?

before the second set
beard buys me a beer
he knows a west texas hellscapes awaits

grinding metal and sunshine
there's enough gas stations
to make it across the endless
without having to bury a roadside shit
like a cadillac on the lbj ranch

you know he used to do his business
in the oval office with the door open
negotiating votes trousers around ankles
it was the sixties then
nobody dared light a match

I'm drunk when band girlfriend arrives
trade out my audience membership
these highways made far more sense sober

for miss woodchopper

it's a sawdust morning
seed pods swept off lover's lane
fall into a low tide river
once home to pirates

the salt sulfur well capped
the courthouse sleeps
there's five for a dollar
gently used bvd's filling
banana boxes in the thrift store

every year the lumberjacks come
push the motel past capacity
car and chainsaw fumes
drift to parades and fireworks
these mountains once again
find something to live for

in the local market
where products are so hyper local
they have the makers telephone numbers
written in careful and shaky pen

a blonde in a pink floyd t-shirt
bored at the counter says
she's gonna be miss woodchopper
this is her year
besides, she could use the win

a stunned communion

he says
it's a winter day in arizona
except it's clarion
this river snakes between
glacial ravines
the last of color
october's days are numbered

he says
they built this village as the titanic sank
it's been his for thirty years
front end loader idles
he's an old man now

he says
seventy-three
whitetail in headlights
we're all in the weeds
I'm closing in on fifty
that doesn't seem strange
until I say it out loud

not that I have trouble
accepting mortality
the reason I'm immersed
in beech and porcupine
looking for a moment
to live in lost

it's more weight

how time feels accumulating

how the body accepts age

a stunned communion

that boxcar life

missoula ain't a big place
if you carry a pizza across the city
no one will notice except the big
white m landscaped on the mountain

chill in the air stays into may
the road over lolo pass clear
but one step beyond winter is still untamed

motel door open
east broadway all evening hush
if I had a pistol I'd shoot the clock

the oldest bars in montana
don't have jukeboxes or tvs
the old west nudes
the remington's as rockwell
slowly die out
another lie of the true west

this hobo stacks his pack
pays in change for moose drool
thunders his story

he is north wind along the rails
teeth chattering on the spine
of the canadian rockies

heading for a springtime
in alaska that's forty below

he ain't jack black
this ain't *you can't win*
no one wants to hear
that boxcar life
no one wants to hear
hallelujah I'm harry mcclintock

after I cross the deep blue sea

(for geechie wylie)

south of empty bar of ghosts
in a town called driftwood
a bend in the road, a bull elk
seven points, grace in graze

dead stop screech to abandon
no one around anyway
turn down archaic blast
last kind word blues

I p'fer just leave me out, let the buzzards eat me whole

a slow memory
picture in picture
an afternoon in north dakota
walk between buffalo
whistle pig popups
massive clouds, still blue sky
maybe heaven never happened

I may not see you after I cross the deep blue sea

I look deep in that bull's eye
I see the universe
all of the universe
I can't see any trace of me

this ghostly ambience

stop me if you've heard the one
about the pregnant waitress and the zamboni driver

yeah, I can't think of the punchline either
what do you expect holding my breath is a new skill
like spiritualism, I practice it sparingly

I'm trying not to think about the soul of a prime rib
     dinner
trying not to notice my former self at the bar
waiting on another beer
then a photo of an illuminated zippo sign
before he shuffles up to buffalo to catch a predator

ever wonder if leon czolgosz got into heaven?

pregnant waitress says
she still hopes they're here in twenty years
the sentence was innocent
now it's dead on the floor

I would go through the stacks
for another conversation piece
but fuck all, sometimes it's best
to leave it there dead

there's a sunset out there
where american flags outnumber people
I should strike up conversation with my addled sense
of wonder

pregnant waitress offers another beer
suddenly dusk is nonsense
suddenly american flags are nonsense
I missed this ghostly ambiance

the age of understanding certainty
(for mike james)

I remember murfreesboro as
seconds speeding towards coyotes
summer night state lines
sam phililps found his way to the sun
I was, still am, looking after ghosts
that evening it was uncle dave macon
the moonshine soaked dixie dewdrop

mike, they're reading your poems tonight
but it's not yr voice, I'm translating
yr words through filters
the mischief is missing
the timing that signals
your sense of wonder is off

lightning flashes
I'm lost in autumn nights
1999 and summerlea street
three blocks and almost twenty five years
that woman and I stayed in touch
now she's married with cats

this is where the cumberland washes in
the stones river watershed feeding
that night in nashville
2019 before the sea changed

time driving bumper cars with abandon
and here I've just passed
the age of understanding certainty

another reading gone in seconds
another saturday coffee shop
goes off to cash in its drink chips
for a taste of something harder

I'm looking ahead through dusk
michigan maps on the seat
switch on the headlights
asphalt reflects street lights
it seems the rain may have stopped

the bag lady of boone

black snake around her wrist
copperhead around her cane
she appears where
curiosity and superstition call

she weaves tales of main street
ancient days framed in black and white
trysts with grandfather mountain
flash in her lightning eyes
she's dreamed ursa
relegated her to the sky
stars are atoms escaped from bone

she feeds on energy
the consciousness of evening
takes all as she passes
leaves a stolen sweet white trillium
the smell of green apples in the air
only the voice of creek remains

four stanzas for larry

still in street clothes
drinking coffee in an all-night diner
at the edge of rural america
should be repeating philosophy lessons
bailed on in favor of nervous breakdowns
lungs steeling courage for another fiberglass night
I found the beats that year
reading *her* sprawled across a booth
maybe a fever dream

in the basement of a prestigious american university
that I wasn't smart or rich enough to attend
recovering songwriter returns to poetry
lazing into longer songs to read
coney island of the mind
twists and turns, hairpin stanzas
foster transitions, free-form experiments
at the bottom of a radio dial

I had been in a car for seventeen days
with an alcoholic who was realizing
how far he was from home
when I hit the ground in san francisco
there wasn't sun or maps
the sites didn't matter as much as
not seeing the world as seventy mile streaks
I waved to the church of john coltrane

blocks away from city lights
a homeless man pisses on a tree
I lose my resolve altogether
the poverty of this place
another city dissolves

somewhere in virginia
she says she used to live
with a woman whose mother
was engaged to ferlinghetti
he still called once in a while
there would be messages
on a tablet next to the phone
larry called

the era of poorly shod

a crown of thorns
in a red roof parking lot
in tom raper country
leaves the faithful
stranded in dusk
a good blacksmith
is hard to find

this is the era of poorly shod
of lame horses
of forgotten saint mosaics
and grande margaritas
all relics to be cast
aside with ease
she calls me amigo
like fourteen months
have been kept under glass
hermetically sealed against
a rigorous sense of time

there are no work crews
to exchange disillusionment for cerveza
no hymns sung by the high
and hundred proof choir
I sit among tv's
watch slushie machines whirl

the white river and light rain
sound the same
no matter the month

in parking lot lights
swarms of wings beat
intermingle in halogen rainbows
another lonely melody
telegraphed across this sweet night
it sounds like hoagy carmichael's stardust

then tequila kicks in
my teeth sound
like charley patton's guitar

some great speckled crash
on the highway

inspired by mushrooms
walking across my shirt
she asks about dmt
our eyes turn to saucers
wide and black
conversation sans words
what goes on
on the other side of the sky

she hands over a sweating bag of chicken
the 66 highway outside
rolls as art deco ghosts
grope for the last oxygen

I, psychedelic voyager
trace limestone cliffs crests
fish for line violations
signs flash
memphis or tulsa
it ain't like there's a wrong answer

roy acuff has got it all right now
crackling radio, some great
speckled crash on the highway
turkey vultures ain't never
paid no mind to praying

with no signal

stars glow

like times beach in its prime

look up through the night

see that armadillo

on the ridgeline

backlit in moonlight

be still a moment now

listen to that fucker howl

out of time, out of season

we brought constellations
from our corners
of this tattered country
these nonlinear notes
pasted across a massive sky

shake off isolation
the burdens of middle age
there is warmth here among poets
tall tale memories chased
with cornucopias of fried chicken

we'll greet the gasconade at dawn
black wasps on patrol
as river rumbles
low blood and brown silt

on the deck
circled by labradors
we build the frame of the day
this celebration, this comradery

there is evidence of constellations
found in our words
as they echo across the ozarks
out of time, out of season

el gallo

crows across a still ink black night
caws answer as shed door creaks open
gasconades to scattered headlamp breakers
flourishes a gas station neon hymn
cries cheers as margaritas raise
rhapsodizes these mad poets
as stars from its belly
belch to burn down bunting
the universe recreated
a nova cataloged in glass
clinging to lightning's braid
a tin heart heard in distance of hours
a faint pulse here at the end
of the industrial revolution

sunday morning abandoned

I pluck two liberty caps
outta my eyes
leave 'em on the counter to dry

victor is up
chalk in hand
he recreates last night's sky
interpretations of constellations
mythology is a personal thing

on the donut
I fall out of foothills
dead armadillo berms
blackguard rearview clouds

rolla, the big box is open
but the garage is a victim
of the great resignation

with space dust patience
I stare down a big bay door
project my own night sky
morning mycelial meditations

a woman collects trash
wonders about my appointment
I tell her I don't mind the wait

in her best southern drawl
my wait is, has been futile
those doors ain't meant for openin'
sorry for any inconvenience

on the donut again
remnants of storms
steam harvest fields
sunday morning abandoned

I don't have the rubber
to reach kansas city
I gotta let this one go
another lame horse
struck by lightning

emphysema highways

she's not an impressive nag
magenta or metallic red
worn down by gasconade dust

even with the suspension shot
and no central air
to best this indian summer

she's been topped and pumped
and can shimmy her way
one hundred and eighty miles
across these emphysema highways

she runs on memories
of joyboy jack oakie
california to sedalia
gasping hard in the home stretch
hold on babe downtown
is a hawk's feather away

one secret knock unlocks
blood orange refreshment
this speakeasy is jealous of her
free range in warehouse dusk
all grit and character
go on don't be shy
when you piss next to her
you'll see how she shines

sparks of rustbelt towns

armadillo in the weeds
dazed in autumn sunset
blind into reading

after the speakeasy
stars pour molten metal
sparks of rustbelt towns
fade in kansas city skyline

armed with double cheeseburger
and twenty five milligrams
balance the drugs right
keep the pedal down at the edge of mind

these are riot moments
boisterous stories accumulated
in the tragedy of living
hell, I missed these whirlwind sermons
sawed off unceremoniously
into a world of isolation and uncertainty

as the hours flash on
age plays tag with us
he's the first out
slowing to a stone still statue
face hardened in a gumdrop hit

now as buddha
with short circuited loudspeaker
I think I'm done

redneck flex

there's only so much redneck flex
a good ol' boy can offer
spit in a coffee can
a cluttered dusty auto shop
I roll in a tire that gave up

I have dash lights
to remind me
everything is alright
everything is not all right

hell, I'm good at ignoring warning lights
elsewise I wouldn't bother
pulling these bones out of a drug coma
every fucking morning in search of futility

wet tire trails in the dust
back up the hill
back up on the jack
sweating like a shade tree
wheezing like a carburetor
it's hard under this sun
to tell shot from shod

the great missouri bok choy disaster

poets never tell the real story
of the great missouri bok choy disaster
they never tell how this
should be jesse james
saddling up to trade
silver for whiskey
an armadillo at his side
breathless as it mounts the stool

steve sees miles on us
a sarape fit and decorated
with a bank robbery gone awry
I pick a bullet out of my teeth
leave it on the bar, a souvenir

we board the doors against
a motorcycle gang of skeletons
brains on their empty minds

if there's a distraction
I'll make a break
for the phillips sixty-six
at the edge of town
lonesome as any bus station
on the great plains

I'll take a ticket anywhere
maybe west palm beach
maybe schenectady

if I sold a few books
I might have enough for a pint
something to keep dread down
something to keep company
under bright explosion sky
what's the odds on making sunrise?

a bed of dead lizards

hear that gravel bellied song
that gravel bellied reply
these birds foreign to me flash
flickers of color unrecognized

shelled by a walnut tree
I sit on match sticks, splinters
cows low at that side of the road
sun hasn't broken the ridgeline
soon heat will reach dangerous

I've memorized this same sky
deep in the wings of night
when the only sounds
are cricket's legs
and the slow burn of stars

as night stretches
time is once again
valueless

it's past time to shelter
crawl into a bed of dead lizards
let the swamp cooler
take the sting
out of that thermometer

or see if the tire patch
will handle this sticky tarmac
through one armadillo towns
complete with headless bears
and collapsed eaves

in a roadhouse
I order a gallon of sweet tea
a platter of catfish
let the air conditioner be my spine

if luck holds
beyond mark twain
or the mississippi
then it's keokuk
the sixty-one highway
disappears
the ghosts of iowa
eccentric as howard hughes

the last thunderstorm of summer

link wray reminds me
there's gonna be a revival tonight
the last thunderstorm of summer
high beams on, tailgates my ass
as I wear out the fifty highway

catch a drink of purple rain
tower grove park passes
humidity a thick smog
rising off grand boulevard

pecker peepers and free jazz
flirt with a kiss of whiskey
these punk rock dives
these barbecue sermons
these endless gateways west
I always smell my way
to the mississippi

but not now
these shadows are too long
the alcohol can't pace the loneliness
which is to say I think I'm cashed

let me rest my eyes
catch my breath
maybe a short stack for fortification

before I'm eastbound or down again

bonnie parker heart

I've been dragging this cold front
over three scarecrow states
all I want is a decent meal
                a decent beer

greeted by axel
I wonder briefly why
a seven year old boy
is seated at the bar solo

with the expense of childcare
wouldn't be strange
he's the server's kid
crayon drawn menus
'til shifts end

it wouldn't be strange
his family are regulars
axel wanted to sit by himself
independent or willfull

or maybe this youngin'
has a crush on the bartender
her tight autumn sweater
drenched in a volume of curls

a man next to axel

tosses soft voiced questions
as axel tries for the gold
asks the bartender
to fry him a steak

my food arrives
with cops behind me
they use *gentle* cop voices
axel's mother is looking for him

axel is defiant
cops corral him
into a squad car
boy convict
swept up in a sting
a crown of priors
to break a bartender's
bonnie parker heart

across the auglaize

swept out of a motel
between strip clubs
cornstalk in glass enclosure
lost between the renaissance
and *stag at sharkey's*

another blue period afternoon
worms turned my legs to water
a river of roads flows
western ohio expanse closes
to east cleveland cannonade
I probably ask this too often
but where are you now d.a levy?

once more across the auglaize
into a dead neon diner
to a valley lit brew pub
to a fresh bookstore reborn
you might say I'm collecting hexes
another same old ghost
left to haunt what's familiar

montevideo

morning rush
waitress in flight
miscalculates
bumps sidewall
audible *owww!*

rubs shoulder
order pad in hand
a bruise will bloom
another in a series
another shared experience
patrons see their faces
in the coming of purple
this study in collective pain
still lives of the working poor

we eat down
last night's debt
under a city scene
a small window
into the owner's own
immigration tale

a parade painted
uruguayan flags flow
the movements of cities
as black women

joy their only flag
dance across the street

just a moment
half a world away
a place called
montevideo

on mayfield road
with the motion of autumn
in another country
on the near side of sleep
these dreams called
by their proper names
sit faint as embers

under a paw paw

the armadillo
heaves a heavy sigh
at the next and
last state line

step right up
appalachia is waiting

haggard after
skywriting figure eights
across the midwest

if you need me
I'll be under a
paw paw
a bed of leaves
constellations of seed pods
the cusp of a season
waiting like a fool
for ripe fruit
to fall

hang on skyline

these mountains
these clear daughters of stars
reach to the sky to catch
a falling super moon

here I am stoned witness
mugging with yogi bear
ranger smith can keep his picnic basket
we're rolling like mezzrow
yeah babe, these really are the blues

half baked eyes
drop off consciousness
in a sleeping bag my heart
beats into the earth

wake to cold morning bones
bitter shouts of shattered glass
I drag myself to showers
only to find hope lukewarm

there are no smooth edges
here without hot water
as I suffer, a yellow jacket
shattered glass exoskeleton
dragging across tile floor
toward my truck stop foot

I stand in cold running water
as this bee keels over
it shudders in that familiar way
we all do when the secrets
of consciousness leave us

suddenly this yellow jacket
is only an empty exoskeleton
and I am running water alone

I blast heat to reknit bones
as I chase mist up
this river of spruce
this hang on skyline

with a waterfall I stop
undress an orange
let myself feel like a truck stop
in the first light of morning

someday someone may find
my body at the bottom
of white oak canyon
an empty exoskeleton
with crows for eyes
all the secrets of consciousness
rise in morning mist
then dissipate in a forever blue sky

buttermilk skeleton

the moon is a ghost
buttermilk skeleton
rising against afternoon
I cross from maryland
in search of costal waters
these traditions, these miles
add up still unsolvable

herons fish under loblolly and cypress
these waterways, these estuaries
this sky darkens in gridlock
I walk past the last lights of christmas

a storm blows in
it's voice in each wave
eyes focus on speeding clouds

funny, how we don't remember
our lives before the moment everything changed
years pile up as vacant memories
haunted shelters reveling in abandon
if I look hard I see myself
a wraith vague within the deluge

crowds shout and cheer
as seconds tick away
fireworks open the sky

a small welcome explosion
we ante up once again
prepare for a grand finale

I pour champagne
down my throat, into foam
water ebbs at the edge of my boots
licks sand clean
all these offerings
another series of prayers
here's to the chaos of the universe

Jason Baldinger is a poet and photographer from Pittsburgh, PA. He's penned fifteen books of poetry, the newest of which include: *A History of Backroads Misplaced: Selected Poems 2010-2020* (Kung Fu Treachery), and *This Still Life* (Kung Fu Treachery) with James Benger. His first book of photography, *Lazarus*, as well as two ekphrastic collaborations (with Rebecca Schumejda and Robert Dean) are forthcoming. His work has appeared across a wide variety of online sites and print journals. You can hear him read from his work on Bandcamp and on lps by The Gotobeds and Theremonster. His website can be found at jasonbaldinger.com

This project was made possible, in part, by generous support from the Osage Arts Community.

Osage Arts Community provides temporary time, space and support for the creation of new artistic works in a retreat format, serving creative people of all kinds — visual artists, composers, poets, fiction and nonfiction writers. Located on a 152-acre farm in an isolated rural mountainside setting in Central Missouri and bordered by ¾ of a mile of the Gasconade River, OAC provides residencies to those working alone, as well as welcoming collaborative teams, offering living space and workspace in a country environment to emerging and mid-career artists. For more information, visit us at www.osageac.org

www.ingramcontent.com/pod-product-compliance
Lightning Source LLC
Chambersburg PA
CBHW021326060726
47591CB00006B/1894